hello

SUNSHINe

a little book of happy

fréya eté

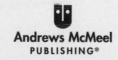

Andrews McMeel
PUBLISHING®

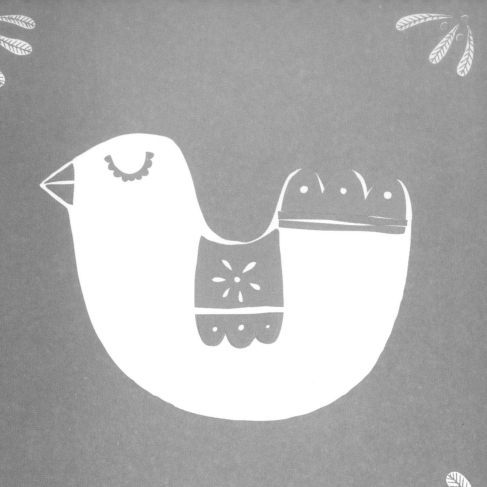

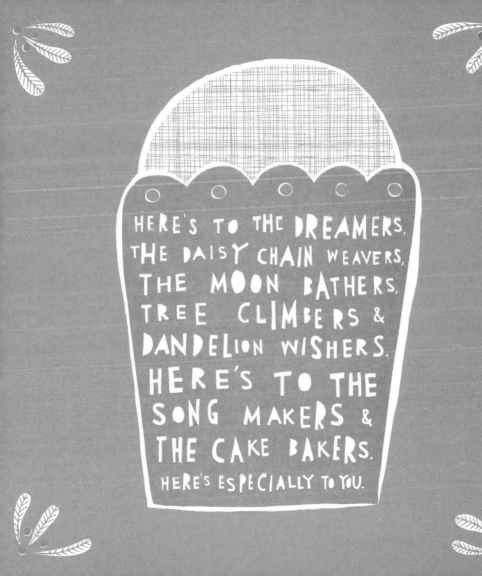

HERE'S TO THE DREAMERS, THE DAISY CHAIN WEAVERS, THE MOON BATHERS, TREE CLIMBERS & DANDELION WISHERS. HERE'S TO THE SONG MAKERS & THE CAKE BAKERS. HERE'S ESPECIALLY TO YOU.

FOLLOW
YOUR DREAMS.
THEY KNOW
THE WAY.

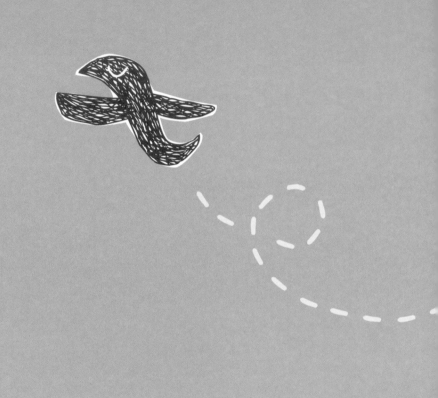

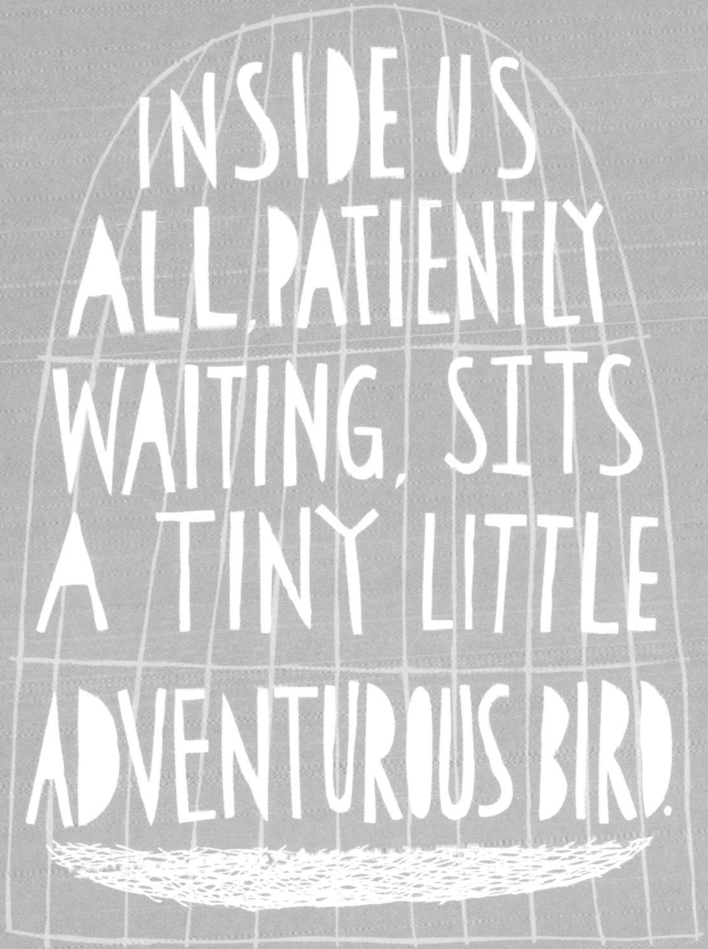

INSIDE US
ALL, PATIENTLY
WAITING, SITS
A TINY LITTLE
ADVENTURIOUS BIRD.

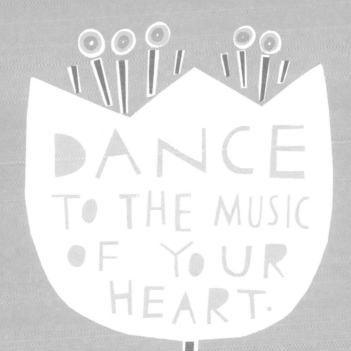

DANCE
TO THE MUSIC
OF YOUR
HEART.

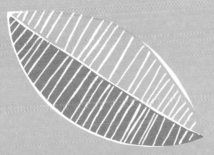

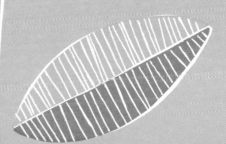

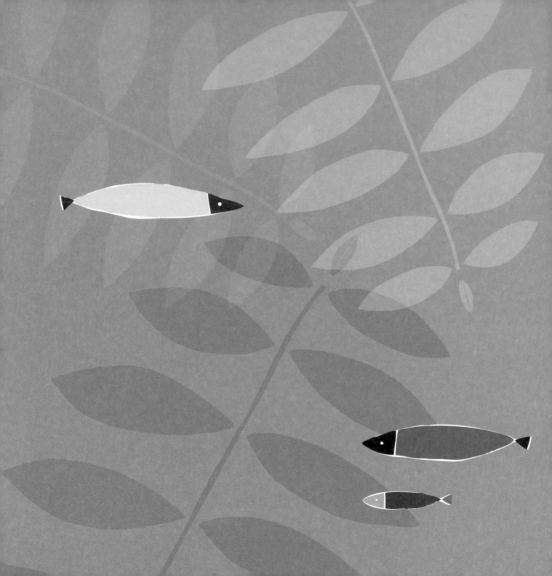

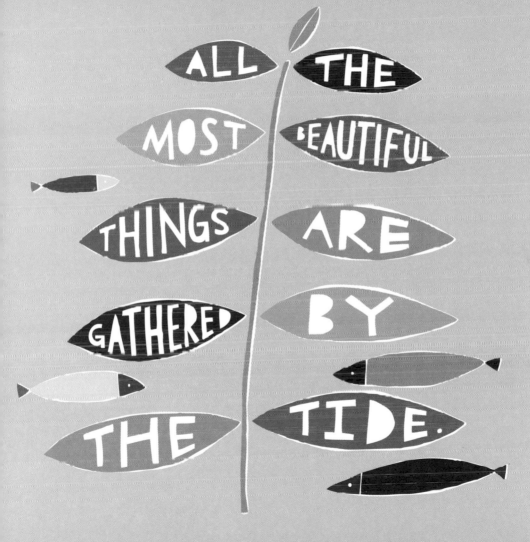

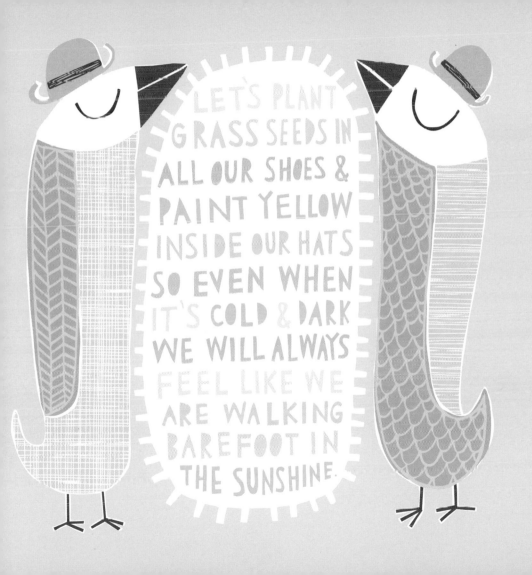

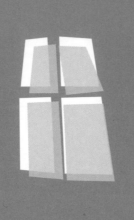

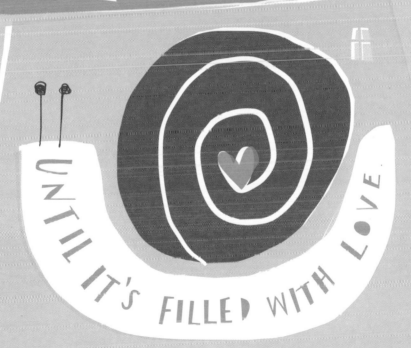

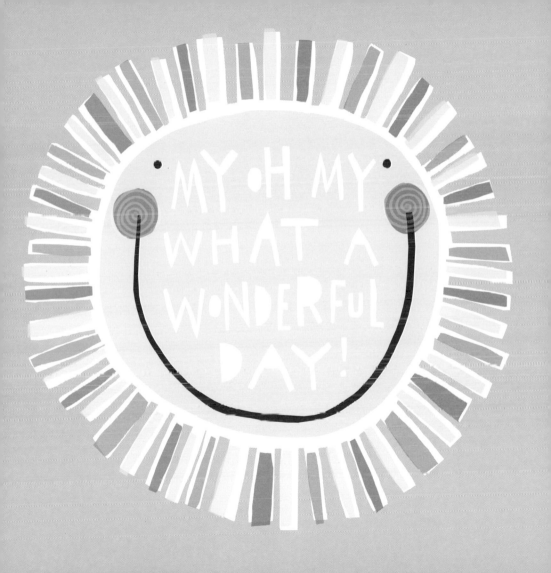

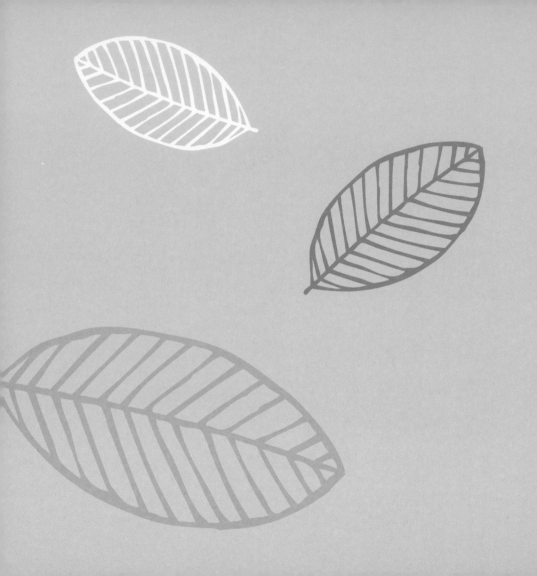

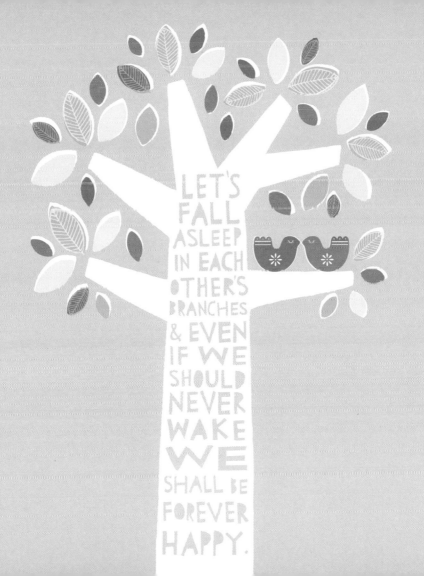

LET'S
FALL
ASLEEP
IN EACH
OTHER'S
BRANCHES
& EVEN
IF WE
SHOULD
NEVER
WAKE
WE
SHALL BE
FOREVER
HAPPY.

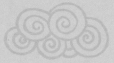

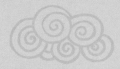

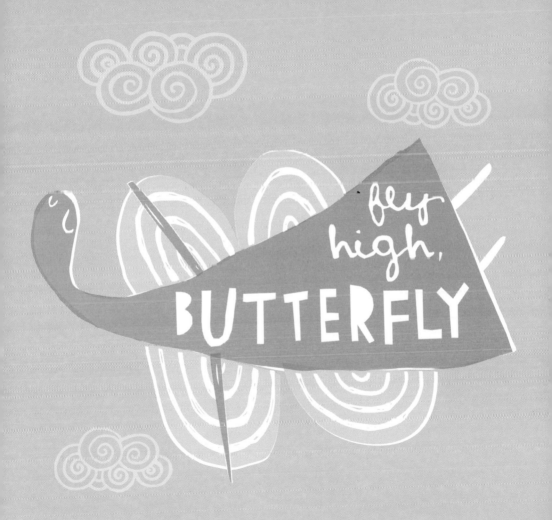

fly
high,
BUTTERFLY

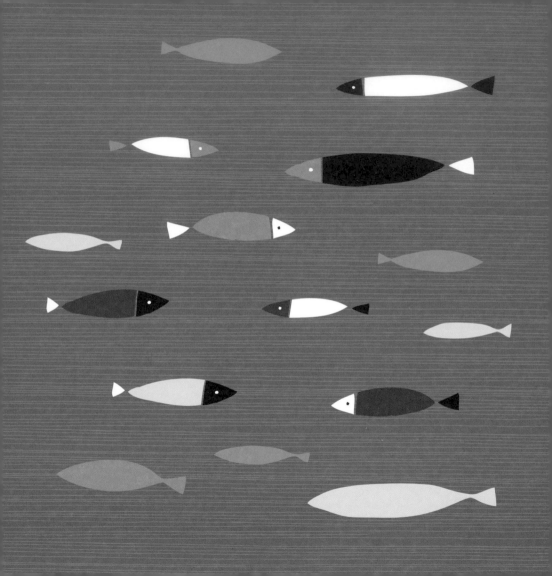

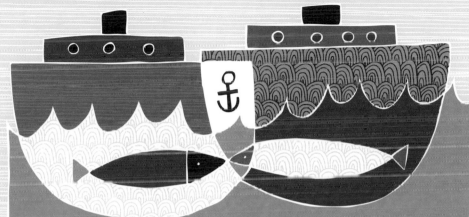

BRAVE WE WERE TO
ANCHOR TOGETHER UNDER
THE MOONLESS SKY
BUT WE SHARED THIS
COMPASS & WE FOLLOWED
THOSE STARS & HERE
WE FOUND OUR HARBOUR.

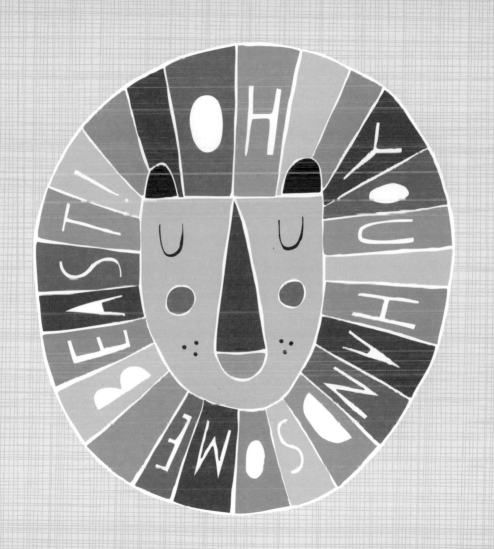

LET'S JUST TIPTOE
GENTLY UPON
THIS LOVELY
WORLD.

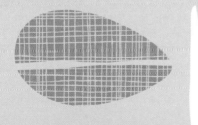
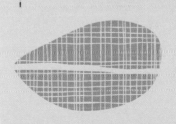

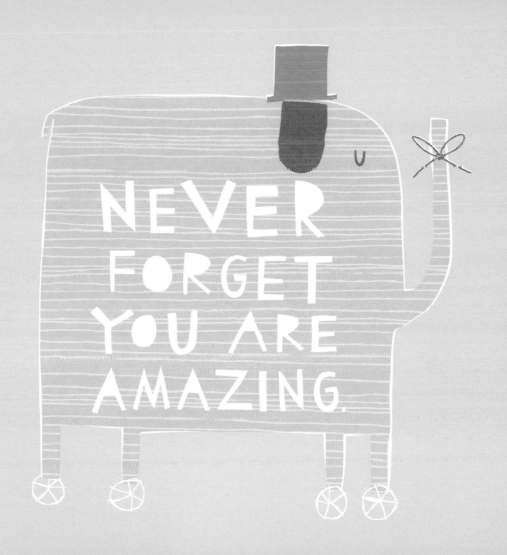

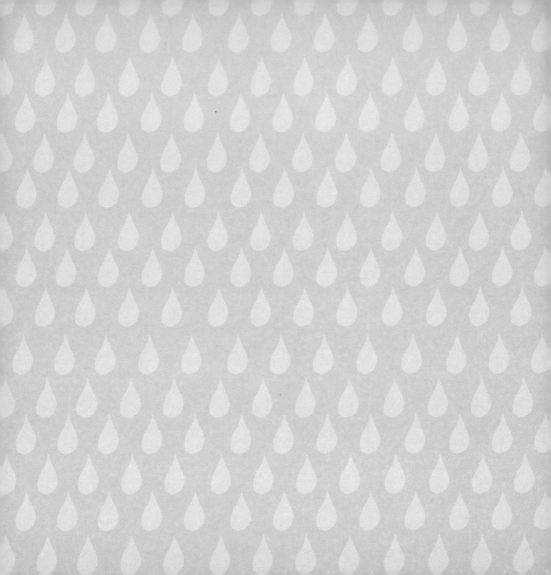

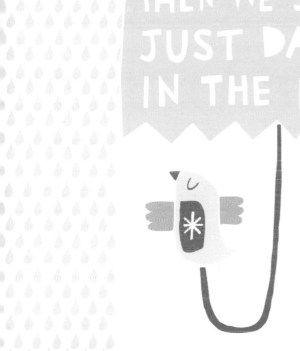

IF STORMS SHOULD COME THEN WE SHALL JUST DANCE IN THE RAIN.

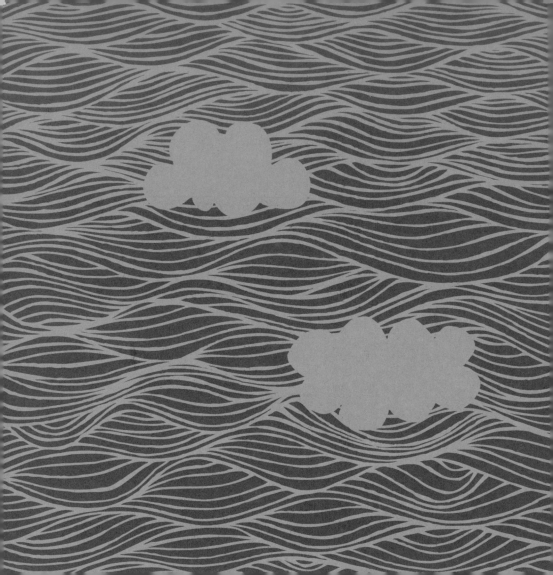

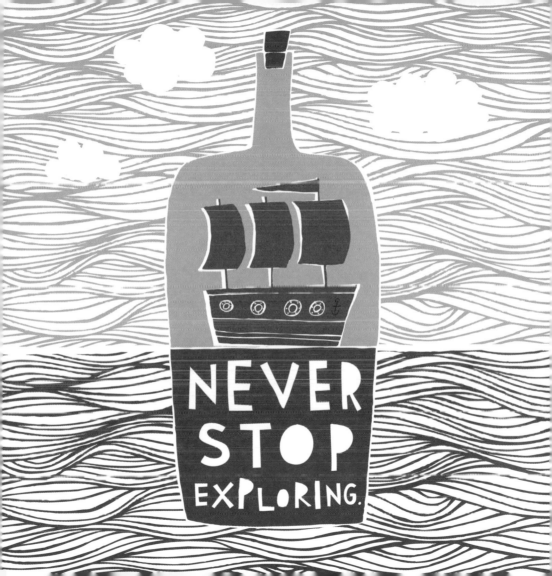

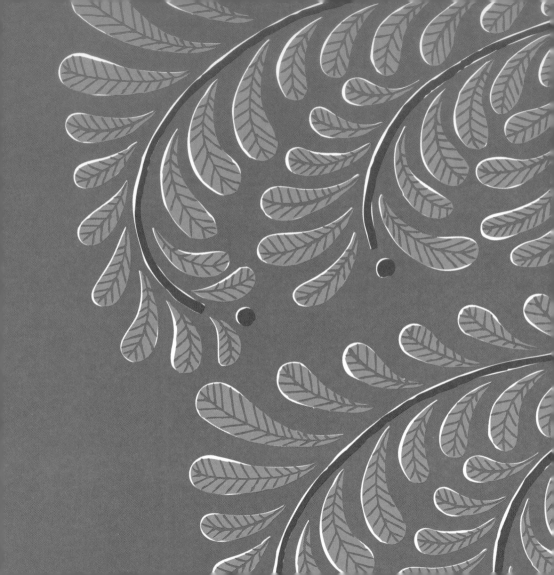

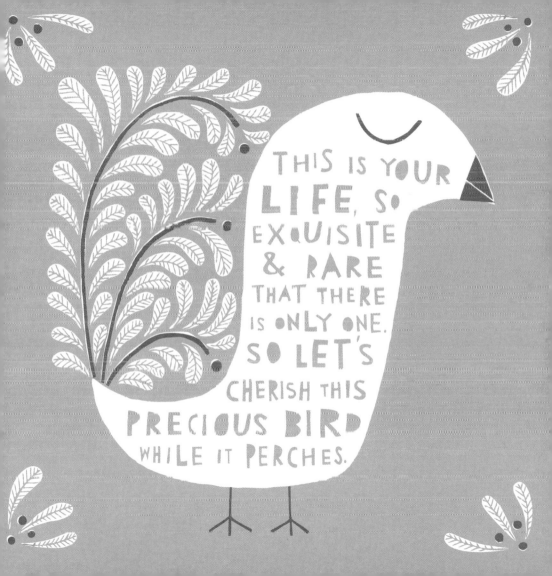

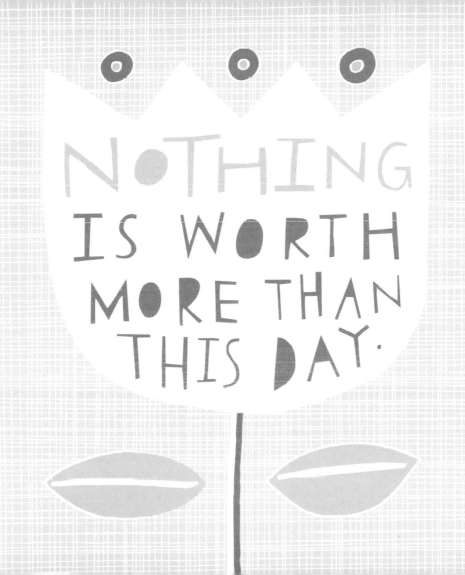

LET'S LIFT THE WEIGHT FROM OUR SHOULDERS & INSTEAD CARRY EACH OTHER'S HEARTS, WITH THE PROMISE TO KEEP THEM SAFE FROM HARM & NEVER FORGET THEIR FRAGILITY SO THEY WILL REMAIN FOREVER LIGHT.

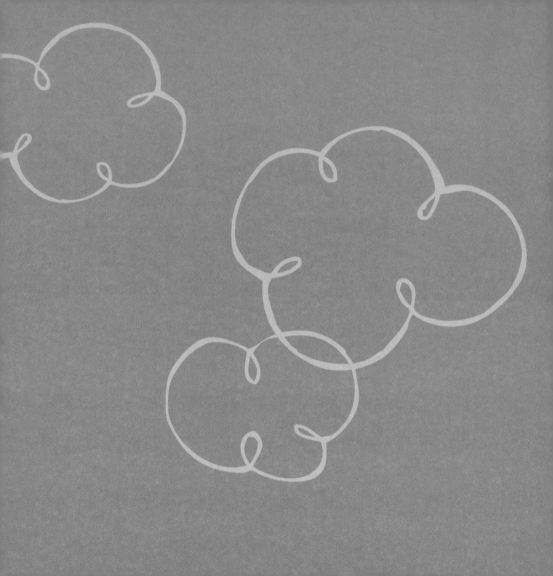

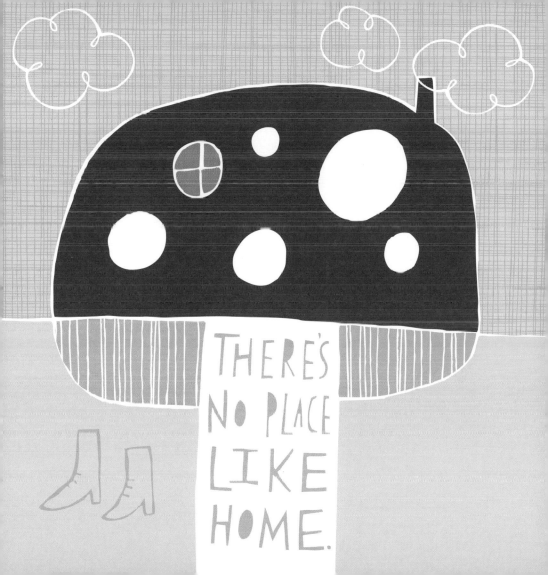

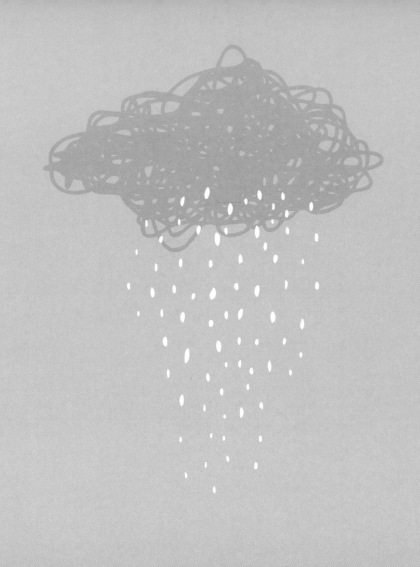

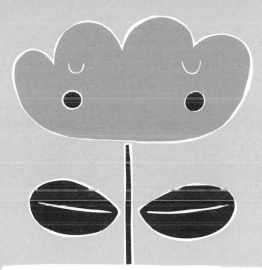

PLANT YOUR
DREAMS IN LOVE
NOT FEAR &
WATER EACH DAY
WITH HOPE
NOT TEARS.

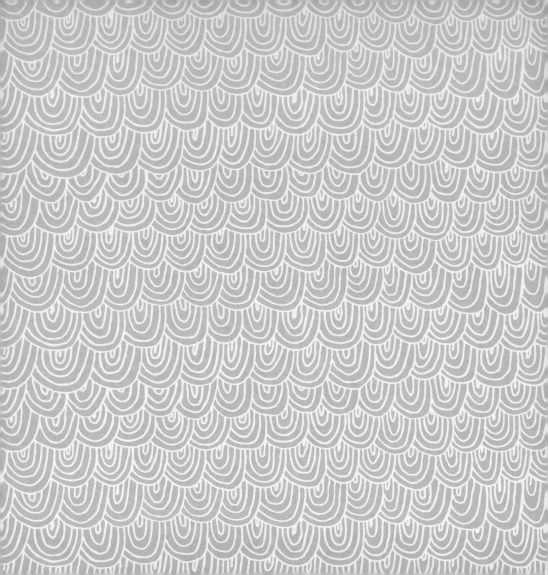

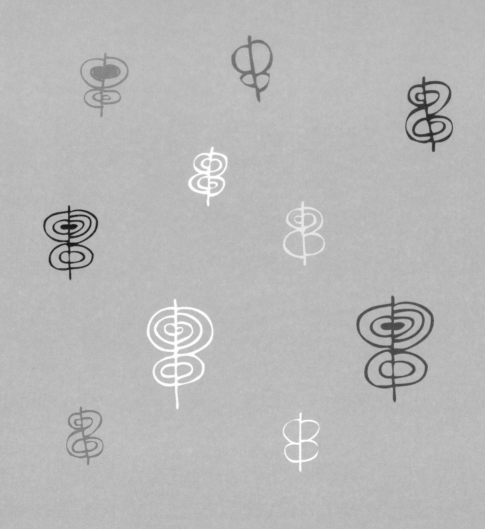

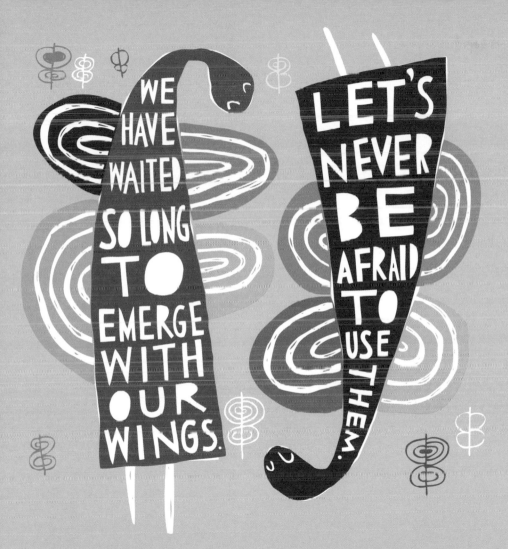

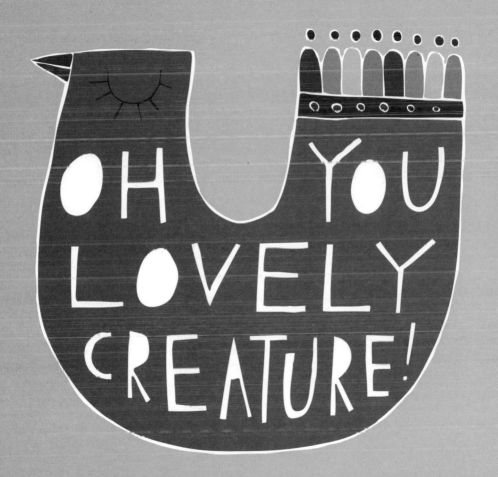

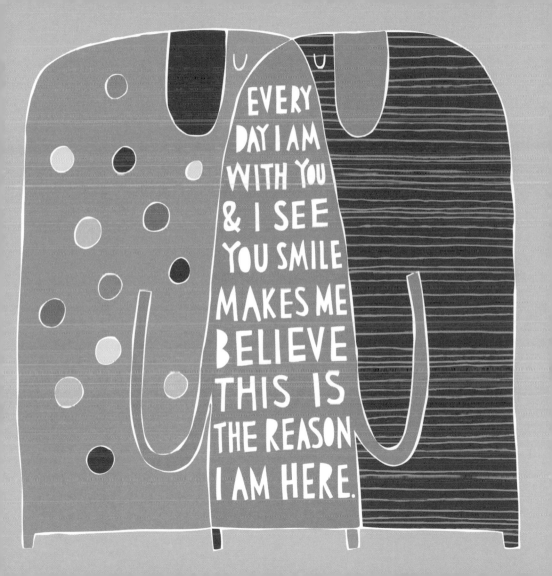

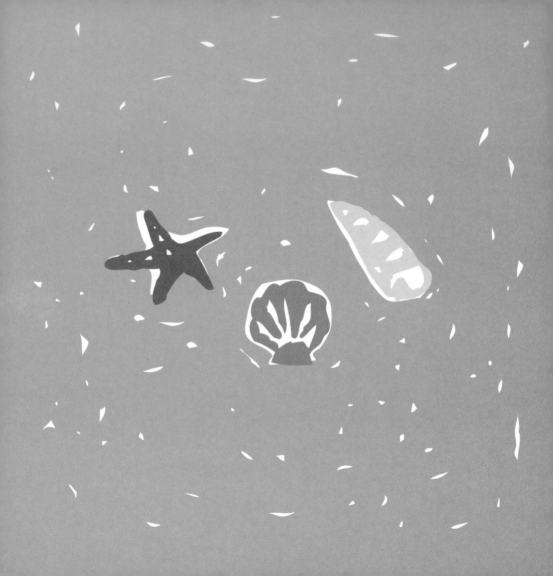

She filled her bath with seastars & driftwood & sat upon its edge & sang mermaid songs that only dogs could hear.

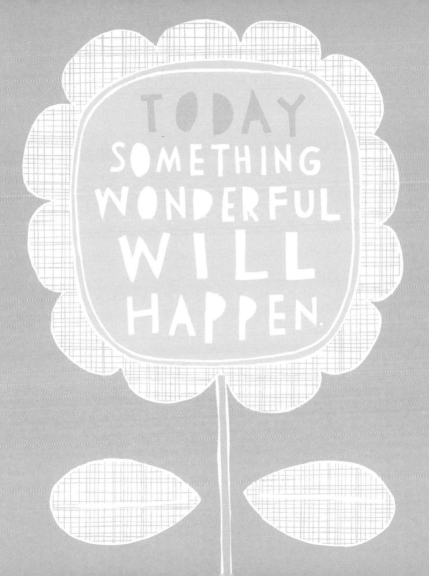

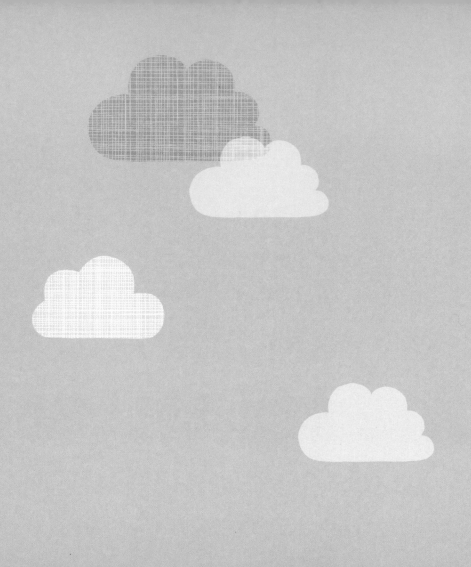

LET'S
LIE IN THE
TALL GRASS
SIDE BY SIDE

&
MAKE OUR
WHOLE WORLD FROM
JUST THIS SKY

& EVEN
IF THAT'S ALL
WE EVER HAVE
WE SHALL FEEL
RICHER THAN KINGS.

NEVER
FORGET
YOU ARE
LOVED.

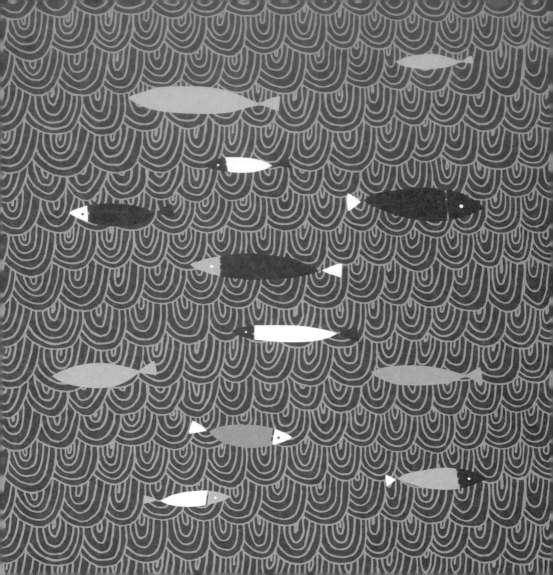

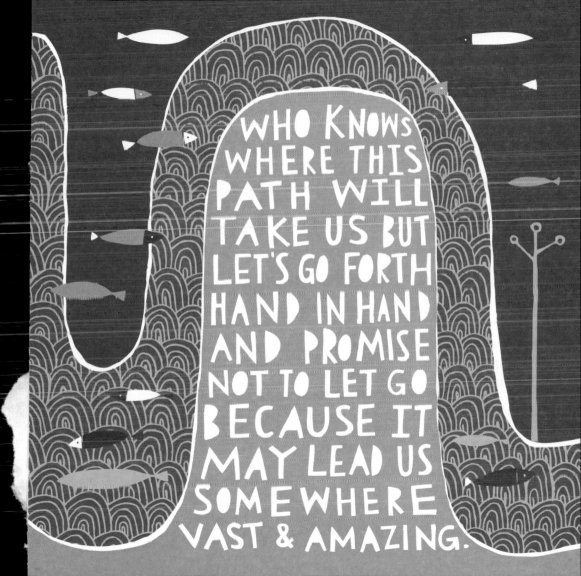

hello SUNSHINE

Andrews McMeel Publishing
a division of Andrews McMeel Universal
1130 Walnut Street, Kansas City, Missouri 64106

www.andrewsmcmeel.com

17 18 19 20 21 TEN 10 9 8 7 6 5 4 3 2

ISBN: 978-1-4494-7412-6

Library of Congress Control Number: 2015951739

ATTENTION: SCHOOLS AND BUSINESSES
Andrews McMeel books are available at quantity discounts with
bulk purchase for educational, business, or sales promotional use.
For information, please e-mail the Andrews McMeel Publishing
Special Sales Department: specialsales@amuniversal.com.